Existential Reminders

Edward L. Hannon

Content

Edward L. Hannon©

Foreword

This book is designed in a unique way; in order to emphasize to the reader the significance of each concept. This book also deals with unfortunate issues, which American society, along with others, will continue to face; if they are going to be socially blind to the common good of humanity as a whole.

Acknowledgement

I would like to thank "SOURCE CONSCIOUNESS" for gifting me the ability to write these collective works; which will be the existential syllabus for tomorrow's potentiality. I would also like to greatly thank all those who contributed to Microsoft Clipart; which helped greatly to illustrate some of the concepts mentioned in this book.

Philosychology

Philosychology (noun) is a study of conscious behavior created by PhTCB (philosopher and teacher of conscious behavior) Edward L. Hannon. This science is a synthesis of empirical psychology along with his philosophies to methodize a practical or practicable solution to resolve the dilemmas, conflicts, or queries that mankind perpetuates upon itself.

Chaplain Edward Lewis Hannon D.D. (Doctor of Divinity)

"For those who are prudent and transparent enough to not give a damn about what others may think, a smear campaign is but a begrudging pedestal of profound acknowledgment; typically, done by others who lack the personal integrity to humbly admit that they are quite impressed."

"One of the greatest evils that humanity has ever perpetuated upon itself was to create an unreasonable sense of utter perfection; which remains totally exclusive to an idealistic narrative of a spurious fable."

"Time offers no permanency to nations that have yet to learn humility."

"As it relates to dealing with others, once you understand your emotional potential, do not allow yourself to become psychologically derailed by passive aggressive behavior that is only meant to keep you destabilized."

"I had to become a broken man; in order to understand an inherent sense of Divinity that is eternally whole."

"Until humanity is willing to ethically change its dietary practices, their level of consciousness and behavior will always be consistent to that of a mere savage."

Be careful when you make an oath to GOD; so your family will not have to grieve because you chose not to keep it.

For those who pledge to defend against all enemies, whether foreign or domestic, make sure that you do not possess a sense of total incompetence; which would, in turn, foster the possibility of such devastating potential.

Fear-based intelligence offers a parochial outlook; which only rationalize existential potential through the shortsighted lens of unnecessary hostility.

There is no greater social threat than a biased mind that pretends to be just.

Intimidation tactics are typically employed by those who lack personal integrity and competence; thereby, they will eagerly pledge their allegiance to that which would offer them a false sense of meritorious status.

Breaking News: Dear Drug Dealers, also including established pharmacists and doctors, I strongly recommend that you change your profession or questionable activities. But, if you choose not to, make sure to check the quality of your products; because, your life may unjustly hang in the balance of a society that chooses to remain unequally accountable for their reckless choices.😆

Sarah Huckabee Sanders Signs Bill To Give Drug Dealers Death Penalty If Their Drugs Kill A User

Forbes Breaking News · 245K views · 2 days ago

Unfortunately, the Voting Rights Act of 1964 (which has to be renewed, appealed and strengthened ever so often) does not afford me the total enthusiasm of a first class voting citizen. So, claiming descendants of the last vestiges of the first culture to acknowledge America's independence, I will reminiscently choose to hoist the colors:

Although, I am quite detached, I firmly support the noble disposition of remaining always kind; especially, in these perilous times. But, as fate or karma continues to remove these willfully rude souls from this plane of existence, by way of a funeral homes' V. I. P. treatment, sometimes I feel that a bit of celebration is in order. And, it is also Biblical😄😝😄!!!

Proverbs 11:10: When it goes well with the righteous, the city rejoices; And when the wicked perish, there is jubilation. (New King James Version)

As long as excuses for some, and blame for others will continue to be a wedge that hinders our collective understanding of humanity's intrinsic potential, then we should logically suspend a sense of total concern; when tragedy discriminates.

Dear humanity, just because you choose to boycott your limitless potential, does not preclude you from being a victim of your own hypocrisy.😀

Well hell, the patriarchal BS of religion has condemned, condescended and suppressed the feminine aspects of existence for millennia; but, somehow wonders why it is faced with a gender crisis, which vehemently does not respect the balance of either polarity.😛

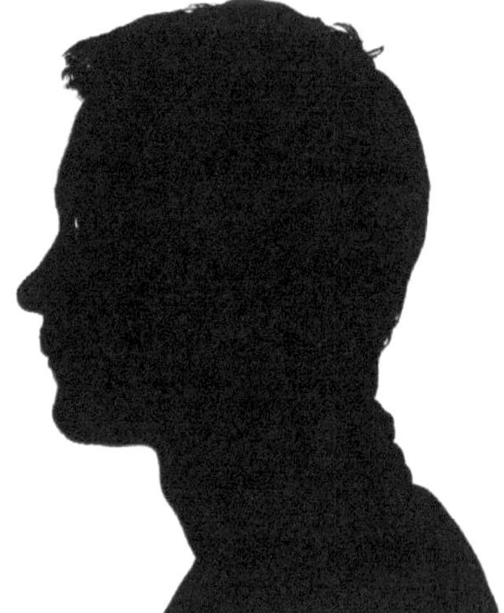

By studying an opponent's inconsistent sense of total hypocrisy, one may prudently develop the tactical prowess to utterly raze that which an opposer has built as a moral safeguard.

For those, who consider themselves hyper-masculine and feel compelled to protest against any beer company, please remember that a beer bottle is more of a phallic symbol than it is feminine; so, to carefully preserve your personal masculinity only drink beer from cups or cans.☺

Many would endeavor to witness the face of GOD; but, may frighteningly withdraw from the mirror, because of inadvertently realizing that in order to do so the limited sense of ego must eventually die.

King James Bible Exodus 33:20:

And he said, Thou canst not see my face: for there shall no man see me, and live.

In a political sense, if you want to be influential, then learn to encourage others in an atomic or individual sense; thereby, you can systemically affect macrocosmic potential as a whole.

Unfortunately, removing all weapons from a society will not stop a mind that is fundamentally violent.

Stupidity can feign a practical sense of necessity; by which, you may find yourself completely enchanted within a precarious state of total belief and acceptance.

The instability of total noncooperation is a provocative force; by which, war cannot resist.

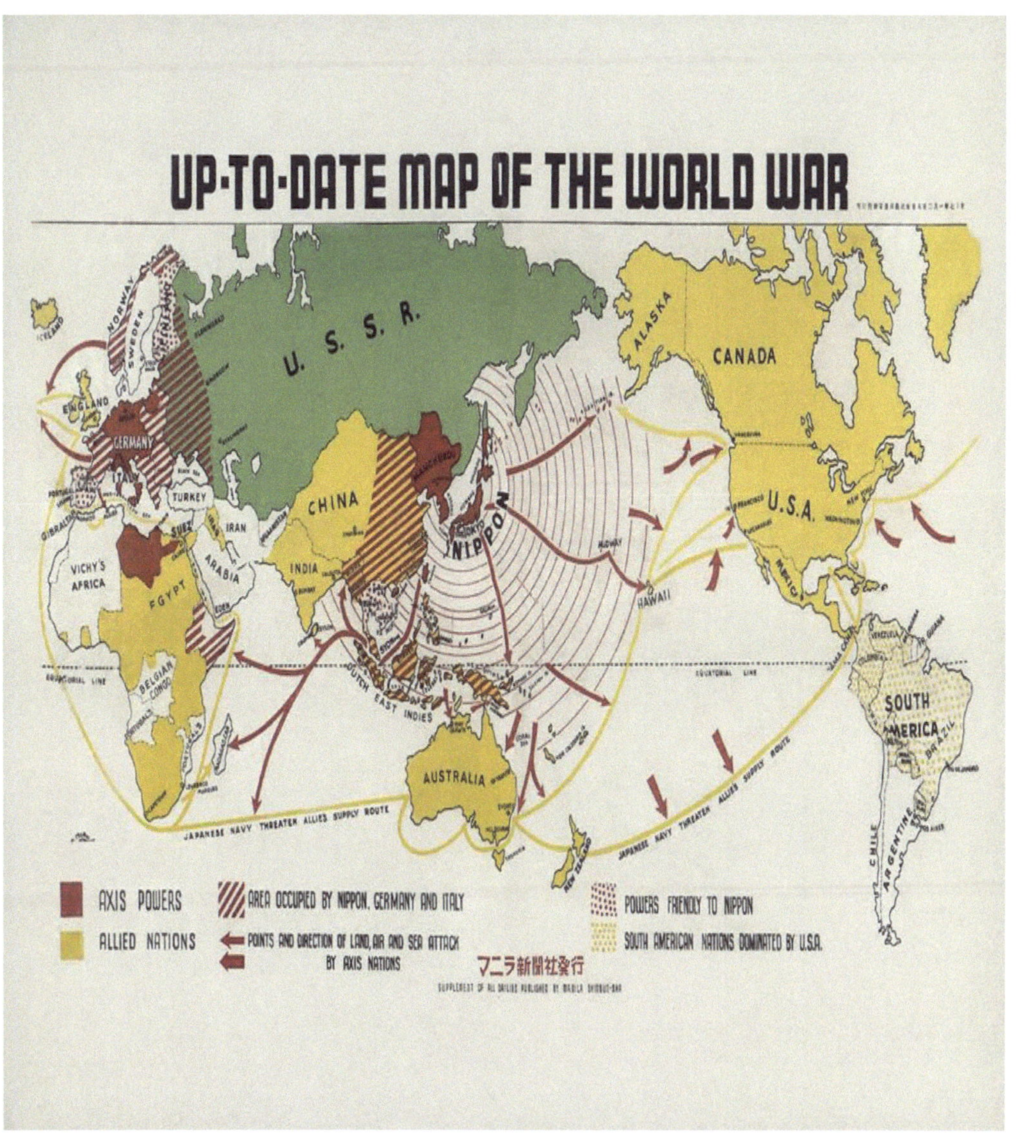

Once you are outside of the social matrix of conventionalism, you may find that the status quo will still seek your personal perspective; in an effort to gauge its existential sense of relevancy.

Humorously, once Mother Nature decides to travel, She typically does not give a damn about the cost of living.😝

One of the greatest existential tragedies is to witness the monster of self-doubt; which could frighten you just enough that you would haplessly run from your utter potential.

Never expect to meet the expectations of those who remain psychologically Ill-equipped to find personal relevance within themselves.

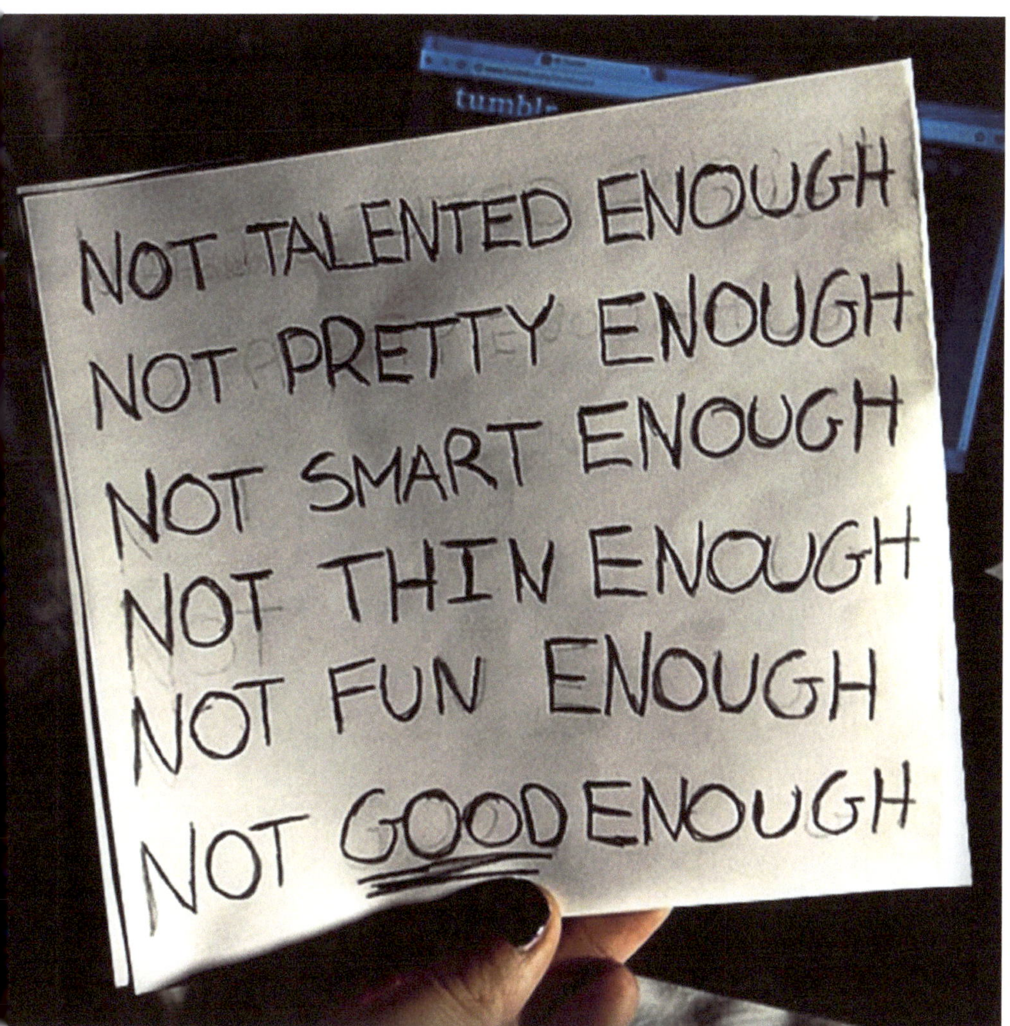

Unfortunately, with all of the drastic cosmetic surgeries and enhancements that many do, in an effort to maintain or attract personal attention; it still does not impress the undertaker enough to either make them a mortuary calendar model or offer a glamour discount.😛

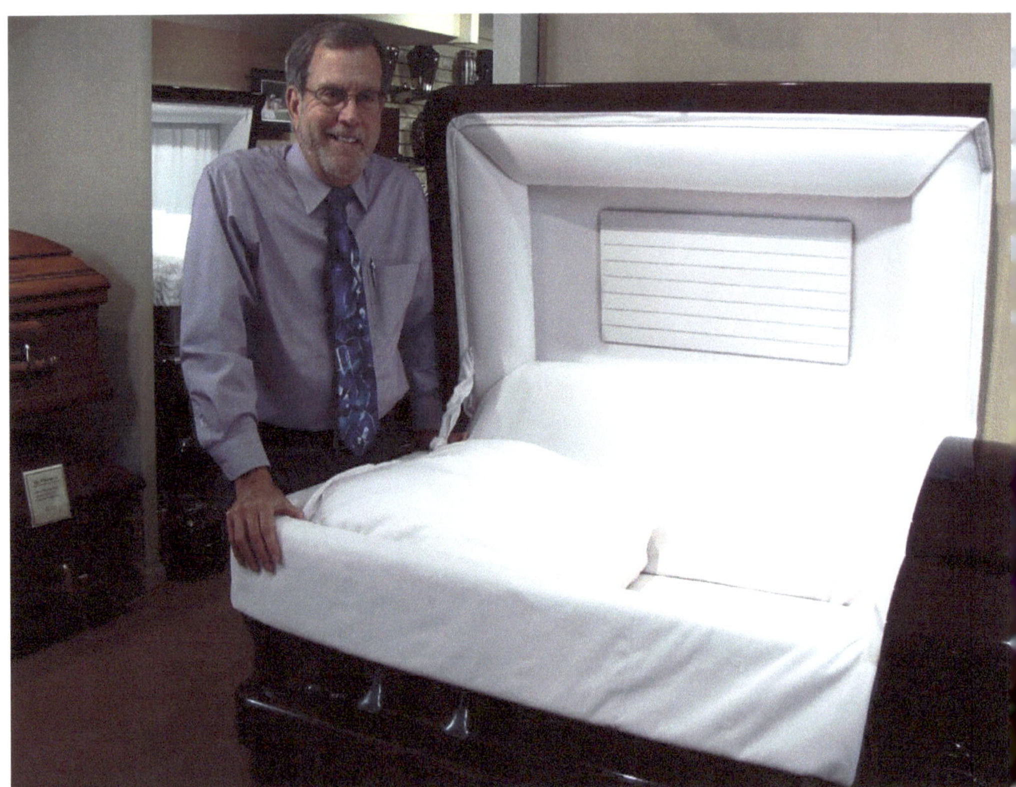

Those that are prone to secretly spread lies are typically under a contagion of unrest; which can only be remedied by those who are poised enough to be glaringly transparent.

Do not fear passive aggressive threats from a foe who vehemently profess to stand and fight; especially, if you have strategically decided that you would lose everything, at the rewarding cost of their complete demise.

Never allow yourself to be coaxed into revealing the power of your personal potential, by those who are only seeking a spectacle; lest, you find yourself under the frivolous whims of their desire to be solely entertained.

To those who innately realize their existential status of total immortality, if ever threatened by the insubstantial prospect of death, make it your personal task to personify that ghosts do exist.

There is nothing more noble than to prudently assume an accursed disposition; in order to strategically protect the just from being a victim of profound Ill-intentions.

Humorously, there are those who profess to follow the reality of a Christ; and there are those who are sent to gladly remind them why they should. Hence, I would prudently take the latter approach.

Afterthought

My Collective Works:

Immortal Tomorrow

The Acquisitions of the Spirit: The Rise of Vibrational Consciousness

The Consciousness of the Spirit: Philosychology: Edisms and Edimous Concepts

The Path and Pinnacle of Consciousness

The Reinforcement of Consciousness

There is Nothing, but the Fractal Nature of GOD

To Serve and Protect

"Day by Day" Oracle Book Reading: "First Pick a Number! (1-31)"

From Nothing

Mystic Consciousness

Nothing More to be Said

Quantum Discourses about the Reality of Energy

Sapient Awakening: The Rise of HOMO-DEUS

Sapient State: The HOMO-DEUS Consciousness Realized

Sapient Tomorrow: Risen Angels and Respectful Demons

Sentient Being

Sentient Comprehension

Sentient Reasoning: A Small Book of Occult Revelations and Mysticism

Sentient Understanding: Mastering One's Demons

Thank You, Chaplain: For The Uncomfortable Truth

Life is but a song:

Who Will

In the perils of my mind

Seeking answers etched in time

For seeing only ill-illusions

Blinding me from my resolutions

Chorus
And I have to ask,

Who will shine when the sun refuses to

Who will stand when they're afraid to

Who will give not asking to do

Who will
Who will
Be this noble few

What can I aspire to be

While fear is consuming me

Instability of my situations

Give avenues of desperation

And I have to ask,

Who will shine when the sun refuses to

Who will stand when they're afraid to

Who will give not asking to do

Who will
Who will
Be this noble few

I have to learn how to release

Pressures of what I know can't be

I must stand for a cause

Even if my fate is to fall

Chorus
So I ask,

Who will shine when the sun refuses to

Who will stand when they're afraid to

Who will give not asking to do

Who will
Who will
Be this noble few

Chorus/Repeat

© Edward Lewis Hannoh

5/28/06

If It's Love

I come in question about our relationship

Because we undeniably know that there's a slip

We no longer talk for fear of blame

Truthfully I know you share this pain

We proclaimed our love would survive the worst of time

So understand why my concern is if…

If it's love
If it's love
Let us not depart

If it's love
If it's love
Let us do our part

If it's love
If it's love
For the sake of love

Our hearts are as empty as space on the wall

Not facing this problem we're destined to fall

The way we carry on we will not cope

But my mind deludes me with notions of hope

We proclaimed together our love would endure the test of time

And I know you will understand why my thought is if…

If it's love
If it's love
Let us not depart

If it's love
If it's love

Let us do our part

If it's love
If it's love
For the sake of love

Baby I believe in you being oh so true

Not looking for another trusting in you

Only through devotion love can be strong

So can we forgive to vanquish our wrongs

Since we proclaimed our love would transcend the best of times

Do understand why my solution is if…

If it's love
If it's love
Let us not depart

If it's love
If it's love
Let us do our part

If it's love
If it's love
For the sake of love

REPEAT: CHORUS

© Edward Lewis Hannon

5/15/06

Existential Concept

Radial Nonlinear Metamorphosing by Kinetically Bypassing Frequency Domain Dynamics

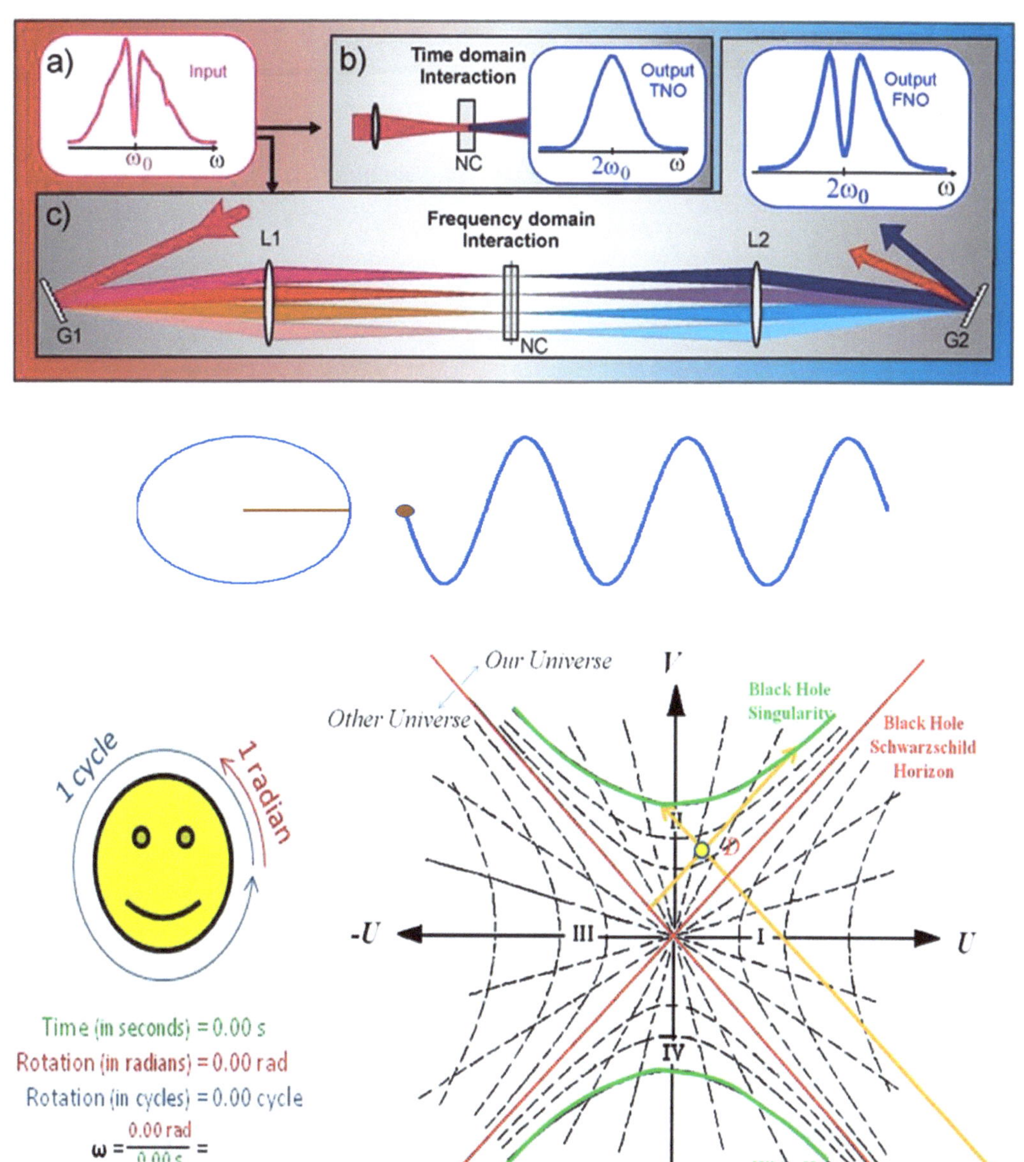